# Z is for Zamboni

## A Hockey Alphabet

Written by Matt Napier
Illustrated by Melanie Rose

Text Copyright © 2002 Matt M. Napier
Illustration Copyright © 2002 Melanie Rose

Zamboni® and the likeness of the Zamboni® ice resurfacing machine used
with permission.

Matt, Melanie, and Sleeping Bear Press gratefully acknowledge the support and
assistance from the following individuals: Steve Shutt, Craig Campbell, Paula
Jensen, and Colin, Jason, and Benjamin Winn.

## Sleeping Bear Press˚

315 E. Eisenhower Parkway, Ste. 200
Ann Arbor, MI 48108
www.sleepingbearpress.com

© 2005 Sleeping Bear Press is an imprint of Gale, a part of Cengage Learning.

10 9 (case)
10 9 8 7 6 5 (pbk)

Library of Congress Cataloging-in-Publication Data

Napier, Matt M.
Z is for zamboni : a hockey alphabet / by Matt M. Napier; illustrated by Melanie Rose.
p. cm.
Summary: Each letter of the alphabet introduces a fact about the game of hockey.

**pbk** ISBN-13: 978-1-58536-238-7        **case** ISBN-13: 978-1-58536-065-9

1. Hockey—Juvenile literature. 2. Alphabet books. [1. Hockey. 2. Alphabet.] I.
Rose, Melanie, ill. II. Title.
GV847.25 .N36 2002
796.962—dc21                          2002004303

Printed by Bang Printing, Brainerd, MN, 5ᵗʰ Ptg., 09/2010

As a special tribute to the North American origins of the game of hockey,
we have chosen to use the Canadian spelling of selected words.

Can you find these words? How many did you correctly guess?
Check your results against the answers on the last page.

A is for Arena.
The game is played in here,
a building where the fans all gather
to clap and boo and cheer.

An arena is a large area where people gather to attend sporting events, concerts, or shows. Because hockey needs a large sheet of ice to be played, all early hockey arenas were outdoor rinks and games could only be played when the weather was cold enough to keep the ice frozen. As people experimented with different ways to make ice, and keep it frozen indoors, it became more and more common to see indoor hockey arenas.

**A** can also be for the All-Star game. This game is held once a year and showcases the best and most talented players the National Hockey League (NHL) has to offer. The fans often pick the team starters, and the location of the game rotates between cities in North America.

A a

Bobby Orr played most of his NHL career with the Boston Bruins as a defenceman, where he was one of the game's most prolific goal scorers and playmakers. He won the Calder Trophy for the league's outstanding rookie in the 1966-67 season. Orr also won the Hart Trophy as the league's most valuable player three times, and appeared in the All-Star game a total of nine times.

Bobby Hull played professional hockey a total of 23 years, in the NHL and the WHA (World Hockey Association), spending most of his time in Chicago (NHL) and Winnipeg (WHA). He led the NHL in scoring three times, was the MVP (most valuable player) twice in both leagues, and was an All-Star 12 times in his career.

B is for two Bobbys,
    with last names of Hull and Orr.
Both were skillful players
    who could truly skate and score.

C
C
C

**C** is for the Coach
as well as for the Captain.
They are respected leaders
who can really make things happen.

The coach of each team is responsible for motivating the players as well as employing the best strategy for his team to increase the chances of winning. Over the years there have been some very famous coaches who were able to turn their players into a winning team on a consistent basis. Daniele Sauvageau led the Canadian women's team to an Olympic Gold Medal in 2002. Toe Blake with the Montreal Canadiens, Punch Imlach with the Toronto Maple Leafs and Scotty Bowman with the Montreal Canadiens and the Detroit Red Wings have been considered among the best NHL coaches of all time.

The captain of each team is the player chosen to be a leader on and off the ice. He is the one who wears the "C" on his jersey and acts as a liaison between the coach and the players. Some famous captains have been Ted Kennedy and George Armstrong with the Toronto Maple Leafs, Jean Beliveau and Maurice Richard with the Montreal Canadiens, and Mike Eruzione of the 1980 "Miracle on Ice" U.S. Olympic Gold Medal team.

Hockey is a very positional game, and each position has its own unique responsibilities. For the most part, centremen try to score goals. The defencemen are usually more concerned with preventing goals than scoring them, although many talented goal-scoring defencemen have played in the NHL, such as Bobby Orr and Paul Coffey. The goaltender (the player in a full mask wearing large pads) is the team's last line of defence: after him, there is no one left to stop the puck from entering the net for a goal.

At the start of every game there are a total of six players on the ice for each team: one centreman, one right winger, one left winger, two defencemen, and one goaltender.

C can be for Centreman
while D is for Defenceman.
The first one tries to score the goals,
the second one prevents them.

Equipment is the word
which we shall choose for E,
important for the players
to stay free from injury.

Over the years, protective equipment in hockey has undergone many changes. Skates, for example, have evolved from essentially a soft leather boot with blades attached, to highly protective, yet comfortably fitting, boots with precision-crafted, mechanically sharpened blades. Believe it or not, helmets were not worn until recently.

Jacques Plante, while playing for the NHL's Montreal Canadiens, became the first goalie to wear a mask on a regular basis on November 1, 1959, and other goaltenders were soon to follow.

Another important item of equipment is the stick. Every player has a stick, which is used to pass and shoot the puck. Players' sticks are all similar, but goaltenders use sticks with a larger shaft and blade to block shots.

E e

A forward can either be a centreman or a winger. There is one centreman and two wingers on the ice for each team at the opening face-off. At the beginning of each game, the centreman lines up at the middle face-off circle against the opposing team's centreman. The referee drops the puck, and the two centremen face off to take control of the puck for their team.

F f

F is for the Forward
who likes to skate quite fast.
He loves to pass as well as shoot
to score a goal at last.

# G g

And **G** can stand for Gretzky,
perhaps the 'greatest' one of all.
When he began to play the game
old records were soon to fall.

Wayne Gretzky is considered by many to be the greatest player to ever play the game of hockey; Gretzky holds over 60 NHL records for scoring and playmaking. Among some of the most impressive records are: most 60-goal seasons (five); most goals in a season (92 in 1981-82); most points in a season (215 in 1985-86); and most play-off points (382 in 193 games). While with the Edmonton Oilers Gretzky led the team to four Stanley Cups in five years. He won the Hart Trophy (as the year's most valuable player) 10 times, the Art Ross Trophy (for the regular season scoring champion) 10 times, and the Conn Smythe Trophy twice (as the most valuable player in the play-offs).

The Hockey Hall of Fame, founded in 1943, originally began as a memorial to those who developed the game of hockey. It officially opened August 26, 1961, on the Canadian National Exhibition grounds in Toronto, Canada. In 1983 the vision was expanded to include a museum, which aimed to recognize and preserve the rich history of the sport. The Hall is home to the NHL trophies including the Stanley Cup. In order to be inducted into the Hall of Fame, retired players, builders (coaches, management, or executives), and referees, must first be nominated by a selection committee, which then votes for the year's inductees. The current Hockey Hall of Fame is located in Toronto's BCE Place and is open to fans of all ages.

H is for the Hall of Fame:
to visit is a pleasure.
Home of the Stanley Cup,
it's filled with hockey treasure.

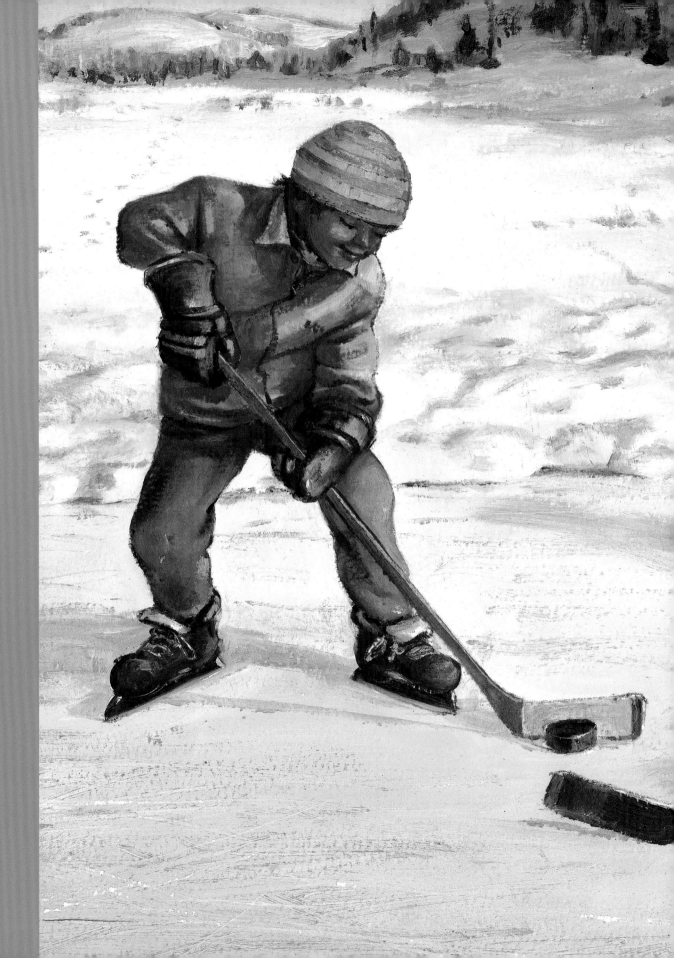

Whether it is called shinny, pick-up, or a scrimmage, kids of all ages play hockey on any type of ice surface—ponds, lakes, backyard rinks, or frozen-over tennis courts in the winter. Obviously, these rinks come in many shapes and sizes; surprisingly, there is no official standard set of dimensions for NHL ice surfaces. Most of the older arenas tend to have slightly smaller playing surfaces, while newer rinks are generally a bit larger. The dimensions of NHL arenas are approximately 200 feet by 85 feet. International rinks tend to be wider, with an average size of 200 feet by 100 feet.

The difference in rink size, as well as the difference in ice maintenance techniques, can give the home team a slight advantage in a game because they have more experience playing on their ice.

For **I** we have the Ice:
like a pond on a winter's day,
where children from all over
can enjoy the game they play.

Most teams have two jerseys: a light-coloured sweater worn at games played on home ice, and a darker one for games played away from their own arena. The sweaters also help players identify their teammates in a game. The style of jerseys has changed greatly over the years, from a heavy woolen sweater, to a lighter, more breathable material. Every hockey team has its own unique colour scheme and logo.

Jersey begins with the letter J—
a team's sweater all its own:
A dark one worn for away games
and a light one when at home.

J j

In 1932, Francis "King" Clancy played on the first Toronto Maple Leafs team to win the Stanley Cup. He came to the Leafs in a trade that has been called "the best deal in hockey" when owner Conn Smythe paid $35,000, which included money he won on a horse race, and traded two players to acquire Clancy. Clancy went on to be named to four All-Star teams, as well as work as a referee, a coach, and then an assistant general manager of the Leafs. He was inducted into the Hockey Hall of Fame in 1958. The King Clancy Memorial Trophy is awarded every year to the NHL player who best displays leadership skills on and off the ice, and has been significantly involved in his community.

K stands for King Clancy:
How much can one man do?
Not only did he play and coach,
he was a manager, too.

**L** is for Lord Stanley's Cup,
every team's true quest.
Its winners hold it high and proud
and proclaim they are the best.

L₁

The Stanley Cup is the trophy awarded to the best NHL team at the end of the play-offs. Lord Frederick Arthur Stanley, Governor-general of Canada at the time, donated it in 1892. The Cup is 35½ inches tall and weighs 35 pounds. It spends most of its time at the Hockey Hall of Fame in Toronto. Each year the name of the winning team, as well as the names of the players, coaches, and team officials are inscribed on the Cup. The first winner of this prestigious trophy was the Montreal Amateur Athletic Association (AAA) in the 1892-93 season. The first American team to win it was the Seattle Metropolitans in 1917. Presently, there are over 2,000 names on the Stanley Cup.

Mario begins with the letter M—
he really plays with flair.
His nickname is "magnificent"
and few players can compare.

Mario Lemieux will be remembered for his dominance in the game while playing for the Pittsburgh Penguins. Over the course of his career, Mario brought two Stanley Cups to Pittsburgh, and won three Hart Trophies, six Art Ross Trophies (as the year's leading goal scorer), one Calder Trophy, and appeared in eight All-Star games. After retiring in 1997, Mario spearheaded a group of investors who saved the team from bankruptcy. He returned to once again play hockey in 2000.

M
m

When Wayne Gretzky played his minor career, he always wore number 9 as a tribute to his hockey hero, Gordie Howe. As he got older, Gretzky adopted the now-famous "99." When he left the game as a player, his number 99 was retired leaguewide.

Gordie Howe was a dominant player in both the NHL and the WHA (World Hockey Association). Known simply as "Mr. Hockey," Howe played his first NHL game with the Detroit Red Wings in 1946. He went on to play for the Houston Aeros and New England Whalers of the WHA before returning to the NHL with Hartford. In a career that saw him set many records for scoring and playmaking, Howe won six Art Ross Trophies, six Hart Trophies, and was named to 21 NHL All-Star games. Gordie Howe was inducted into the Hockey Hall of Fame in 1972.

Now **N** stands for Numbers,
some famous ones you'll see:
There's number 9 for Gordie Howe
and 99 for Gretzky.

When the NHL was officially formed in November 1917, only five teams made up the league: the Ottawa Senators, the Quebec Bulldogs, the Montreal Canadiens, the Montreal Wanderers, and the Toronto Arenas. After the first few years of uncertainty and instability, when some of the teams dropped out and others took their place, the "Original Six" teams found support to succeed in the sport. The Boston Bruins, the Montreal Canadiens, the Detroit Red Wings, the Toronto Maple Leafs, the New York Rangers, and the Chicago Blackhawks were the original six teams and continue to compete in the NHL to this day.

The league's first president, Frank Calder, could not have foreseen the success that was to follow. There are now 30 teams competing in the NHL.

O is for the Original Six,
the first teams in the NHL:
Boston, Toronto, New York, Montreal,
Detroit, and Chicago as well.

Puck begins with the letter P—
black rubber to the core.
It's what the players try to shoot
past the red goal line to score.

# Pp

Made of vulcanized rubber measuring three inches in diameter and one inch in thickness, the puck is the focal object of the game. In order for a goal to count, the puck must completely cross the red goal line that runs in front of the net on the ice; it must not be intentionally thrown or kicked past the goalie. At the end of the game, the team with the most goals wins.

**P** also stands for penalty and penalty box. If a player is caught breaking the rules, he may be penalized (punished) for two, five, or ten minutes, or completely removed from the game, depending on the severity of the action. The player will serve out his sentence in the penalty box (unless he is removed from the game) until his time has expired or the opposing team scores a goal, and he is once again allowed to return to the ice. The entire team suffers a one-man disadvantage for the duration of the punishment.

**Q** is for Quebec
where everyone can say
Les Canadiens have won more Cups
than any others to this day.

Quebec is the Canadian province in which the city of Montreal can be found. The Montreal Canadiens, one of the original NHL teams, hold the record for winning the most Stanley Cups in the history of the league with 23 (not including one win *before* the league was formed). This team also holds the record for most consecutive Cup wins (five).

Two of the greatest players to come out of Montreal were Jean Beliveau and Maurice Richard. Beliveau led the Canadiens to 10 Stanley Cups, and Richard was a member of eight championship teams. Both are members of the Hockey Hall of Fame.

Q q

Referee for the letter **R**
is the word that we shall choose:
The person wearing black and white
and enforcing all the rules.

The black and white striped shirt easily identifies the referee. Traditionally, there are three officials on the ice during every hockey game; one referee and two linesmen. The referee is responsible for dropping the puck at the centre ice, either after a goal is scored or at the beginning of each period, and for calling penalties when a player breaks the rules. The linesmen are responsible for face-offs everywhere else on the ice, and for indicating offsides, icing, and two-line passes.

**R** is also for red line. There are three "zones" in a hockey rink: each team has a zone to protect, marked by two blue lines about 60 feet away from their net, and the middle zone, also called the "neutral zone," is divided by the red line. This line represents the exact middle part of the rink and contains the circle where the referee drops the puck to start each period.

R r

# S s

Slashing is a penalty called when a player intentionally uses his stick to hit an opposing player. The referee will call a penalty of two, five, or ten minutes depending upon the severity of the action. It can be a very serious penalty if the attacking player uses too much force with his stick or hits the other player in an area not protected by a lot of equipment.

And now for letters S and T,
two penalties we meet.
If you Slash or Trip a player:
To the box and take a seat!

Tripping is called if one player uses his stick to intentionally make another player fall. This is a minor penalty, usually served as only a two-minute sentence in the penalty box.

T t

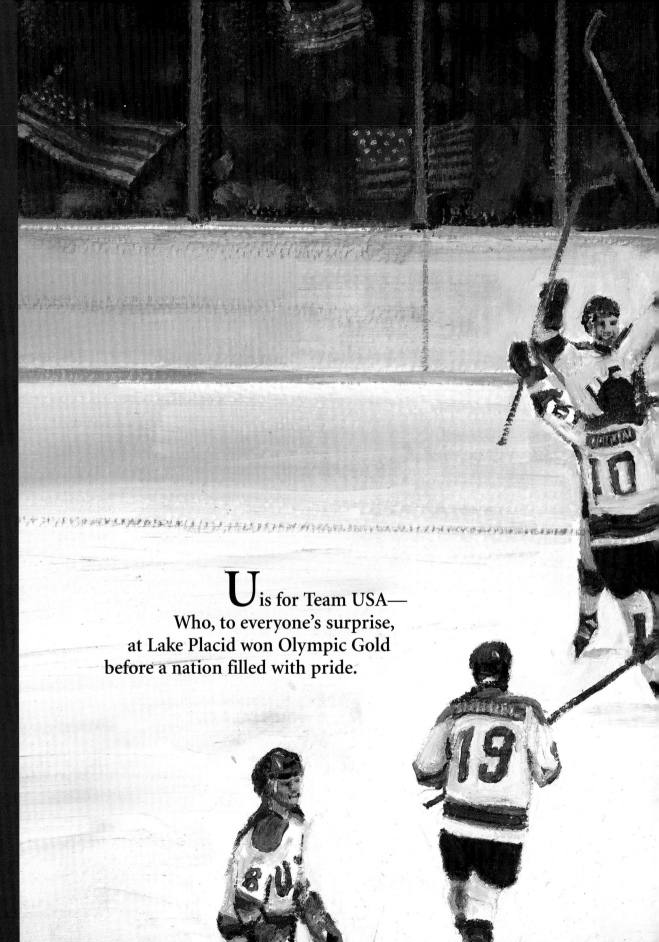

In the 1980 Olympics at Lake Placid, NY, Team USA did the unthinkable. They defeated the heavily favoured Russian team in the semifinals to advance to the gold medal game against Finland. The team then went on to defeat Finland in the final game and brought Olympic Gold back to the United States. Prior to the Olympics, the Russians had beaten the U.S. in an exhibition game by a score of 10-3, and the U.S. was not even expected to win a medal, let alone the gold. Some believe this was the greatest moment in American hockey history and it is commonly referred to as the "Miracle on Ice." Many believe this Olympic win elevated the U.S.'s status in hockey, and changed the way the world viewed American hockey forever.

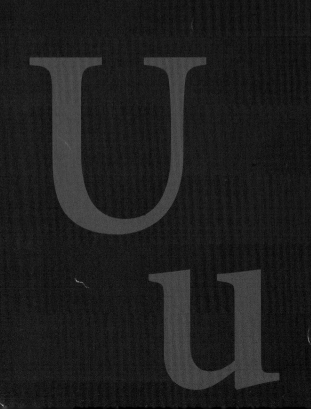

U is for Team USA—
Who, to everyone's surprise,
at Lake Placid won Olympic Gold
before a nation filled with pride.

Vezina begins with the letter V.
It's a very special trophy.
Awarded each and every year
to one outstanding goalie.

In the 1926-27 season, Montreal Canadiens owners Leo Dandurand, Louis Letourneau, and Joe Cattarinich, presented the Vezina Trophy to the NHL in memory of outstanding goaltender Georges Vezina. Prior to the 1981-82 season, the trophy was awarded to the goaltender allowing the least number of goals in the regular season: It is now awarded to the goalie "adjudged to be the best at his position" as decided by the general managers of each of the 30 NHL teams.

Johnny Bower (illustrated) was one of the best goaltenders to ever play for the Toronto Maple Leafs. Bower won the Vezina Trophy twice, and led the team to three consecutive Stanley Cup victories. His number is honoured by the Maple Leafs, and Bower is a member of the Hockey Hall of Fame.

Hayley Wickenheiser is considered one of women's hockey's all-time greatest players. She led the Canadian women's team to a gold medal at the 2002 winter Olympics in Salt Lake City, and, with 10 points, tied for the tournament lead. In 1994, Hayley first joined the women's national team at the age of fifteen, and has won Women's World Hockey Championships in 1994, 1997, 2000, and 2001. In 1999, she was invited to an NHL training camp set up for young rookies and draft picks for the Philadelphia Flyers.

One of the most famous U.S. women's hockey players is Cammi Granato. She is the all-time leading U.S. woman scorer, and the captain of the U.S. women's national team. In 1998 she led her team to Olympic Gold, and in 2002 she was the captain of the silver medal winning U.S. team which lost to Canada in the finals.

W
W

W is for Wickenheiser
and women who paved the way.
Because of them there are more girls
playing hockey every day.

## A Few Other Hockey Terms

**Face-offs** occur at the beginning of each period or after a stoppage in play. There are nine face-off dots on the ice surface: one at centre ice, four more in the neutral zone, and two in each team's zone. At each face-off, one player lines up directly across from an opposing player. The referee or linesman drops the puck and the two players battle for possession. At the beginning of a period the face-off is always held at centre ice: during the period it is held at any of the other eight face-off dots, depending on why the play was stopped.

**Offsides** is a stoppage in play that is called when an attacking player enters the offensive zone before the puck crosses the blue line. When this happens, the linesman blows his whistle and a face-off is held just outside the blue line in one of the neutral zone face-off dots.

**Icing** is a stoppage in play that is called when a player sends the puck from his side of the red line to the opposite goal line. The linesman will blow his whistle and the puck will be brought all the way back to that player's zone for a face-off. This rule only applies in even strength situations and not when a team is serving a penalty.

**Penalties** are called when the referee deems a player has not played according to the rules. There are four types of penalties called depending on the severity of the play: a two-minute minor, a five-minute major, a ten-minute misconduct, and a game misconduct. For a minor or major penalty the penalized player must sit in the penalty box until his time has expired and his team is "shorthanded" one man until he gets back on the ice. This is called a "powerplay" for the other team, as they have a one-man advantage on the ice. There are many types of penalties, some of the more common ones are:

**Elbowing:** When a player hits an opposing player with his elbow instead of his shoulder.

**High sticking:** When a player hits an opposing player with his stick above shoulder-height. This could seriously hurt someone so a penalty is called even if the high stick was accidental and not done in the course of a normal shot or follow-through.

**Holding:** This is called when a player holds onto an opposing player's jersey or stick with his hands.

**Hooking:** When a player uses the stick to obstruct an opponent.

## Matt Napier

Matt Napier was born in Montreal, Quebec and moved frequently throughout North America and Italy with his family before settling in Toronto where he now resides. He currently attends Trinity College at the University of Toronto where he studies Political Science and Ethics, Society, and Law. When not in school, Matt enjoys reading, playing hockey, practicing guitar, and traveling.

## Melanie Rose

Melanie Rose was born in England, and immigrated to Canada with her family as a child. The Canadian Children's Book Centre recently chose Melanie to tour with Children's Book Week 2002 across Canada to promote her first children's book, *M is for Maple, A Canadian Alphabet*. Melanie graduated from the Ontario College of Art. She lives in Toronto with her husband, Darryl, and their two cats, Meesha and Mickey.

| Canadian Spelling | American Spelling |
| --- | --- |
| centre | center |
| centreman | centerman |
| colour | color |
| coloured | colored |
| defence | defense |
| defenceman | defenseman |
| favoured | favored |
| honoured | honored |